THE SHORTNESS OF LIFE
DE BREVITATE VITAE

SENECA

« It is not that we have a short space of time, but that we waste much of it. Life is long enough »

CHAPTER ONE

The majority of mortals, Paulinus[1], complain bitterly of the spitefulness of Nature, because we are born for a brief span of life, because even this space that has been granted to us rushes by so speedily and so swiftly that all save a very few find life at an end just when they are getting ready to live. Nor is it merely the common herd and the unthinking crowd that bemoan what is, as men deem it, an universal ill; the same feeling has called forth complaint also from men who were famous. It was this that made the greatest of physicians exclaim that "life is short, art is long;"[2] it was this that led Aristotle[3], while expostulating with Nature, to enter an indictment most unbecoming to a wise man—that, in point of age, she has shown such favour to animals that they drag out five or ten lifetimes[4], but that a much shorter limit is fixed for man, though he is born for so many and such great achievements. It is not that we have a short space of time, but that we waste much of it. Life is long enough, and it has been given in sufficiently generous measure to allow the accomplishment of the very greatest things if the whole of it is well invested. But when it is squandered in luxury and carelessness, when it is devoted to no good end, forced at last by the ultimate necessity we perceive that it has passed away before we were aware that it was passing. So it is—the life we receive is not short, but we make it so, nor do we have any lack of it, but are wasteful of it. Just as great and princely wealth is scattered in a moment when it comes into the hands of a bad owner, while wealth however limited, if it is entrusted to a good guardian, increases by use, so our life is amply long for him who orders it properly.

---

1. It is clear from chapters 18 and 19 that, when this essay was written (in or about A.D. 49), Paulinus was *praefectus annonae*, the official who superintended the grain supply of Rome, and was, therefore, a man of importance. He was, believably, a near relative of Seneca's wife, Pompeia Paulina, and is usually identified with the father of a certain Pompeius Paulinus, who held high public posts under Nero (Pliny, *Nat. Hist.* xxxiii. 143; Tacitus,*Annals*, xiii. 53. 2; xv.
2. The famous aphorism of Hippocrates of Cos: ὁ βίος βραχύς, ἡ δὲ τέχνη μακρή.
3. An error for Theophrastus, as shown by Cicero, Tusc. Disp. iii. 69: "Theophrastus autem moriens accusasse naturam dicitur, quod cervis et cornicibus vitam diuturnam, quorum id nihil interesset, hominibus, quorum maxime interfuisset, tam exiguam vitam dedisset; quorum si aetas potuisset esse longinquior, futurum fuisse ut omnibus perfectis artibus omni doctrina hominum vita erudiretur."
4. *i.e.*, of man. *Cf.* Hesiod, *Frag.* 183 (Rzach):

Ἐννέα τοι ζώει γενεὰς λακέρυζα κορώνη
ἀνδρῶν γηράντω· ἔλαφος δέ τε τετρακόρωνος.

CHAPTER TWO

Why do we complain of Nature? She has shown herself kindly; life, if you know how to use it, is long. But one man is possessed by an avarice that is insatiable, another by a toilsome devotion to tasks that are useless; one man is besotted with wine, another is paralyzed by sloth; one man is exhausted by an ambition that always hangs upon the decision of others, another, driven on by the greed of the trader, is led over all lands and all seas by the hope of gain; some are tormented by a passion for war and are always either bent upon inflicting danger upon others or concerned about their own; some there are who are worn out by voluntary servitude in a thankless attendance upon the great; many are kept busy either in the pursuit of other men's fortune or in complaining of their own; many, following no fixed aim, shifting and inconstant and dissatisfied, are plunged by their fickleness into plans that are ever new; some have no fixed principle by which to direct their course, but Fate takes them unawares while they loll and yawn—so surely does it happen that I cannot doubt the truth of that utterance which the greatest of poets delivered with all the seeming of an oracle: "The part of life we really live is small."[1] For all the rest of existence is not life, but merely time. Vices beset us and surround us on every side, and they do not permit us to rise anew and lift up our eyes for the discernment of truth, but they keep us down when once they have overwhelmed us and we are chained to lust. Their victims are never allowed to return to their true selves; if ever they chance to find some release, like the waters of the deep sea which continue to heave even after the storm is past, they are tossed about, and no rest from their lusts abides. Think you that I am speaking of the wretches whose evils are admitted? Look at those whose prosperity men flock to behold; they are smothered by their blessings. To how many are riches a burden! From how many do eloquence and the daily straining to display their powers draw forth blood! How many are pale from constant pleasures! To how many does the throng of clients that crowd about them leave no freedom! In short, run through the list of all these men from the lowest to the highest—this man desires an advocate,[2] this one answers the call, that one is on trial, that one defends him, that one gives sentence; no one asserts his claim to himself, everyone is wasted for the sake of another. Ask about the men whose names are known by heart, and you will see that these are the marks that distinguish them: A cultivates B and B cultivates C; no one is his own master. And then certain men show the most senseless indignation—they complain of the insolence of their superiors, because they were too busy to see them when they wished an audience! But can anyone have the hardihood to complain of the pride of another when he himself has no time to attend to himself? After all, no matter who you are, the great man does sometimes look toward you even if his face is insolent, he does sometimes condescend to listen to your words, he permits you to appear at his side; but you never deign to look upon yourself, to give ear to yourself. There is no reason, therefore, to count anyone in debt for such services, seeing that, when you performed them, you had no wish for another's company, but could not endure your own.

---

1. A prose rendering of an unknown poet. *Cf.* the epitaph quoted by Cassius Dio, lxix. 19: Σίμιλις ἐνταῦθα κεῖται βιοὺς μὲν ἔτη τόσα, ζήσας δὲ ἔτη ἑπτά.
2. Not one who undertook the actual defense, but one who by his presence and advice lent support in court.

CHAPTER THREE

Though all the brilliant intellects of the ages were to concentrate upon this one theme, never could they adequately express their wonder at this dense darkness of the human mind. Men do not suffer anyone to seize their estates, and they rush to stones and arms if there is even the slightest dispute about the limit of their lands, yet they allow others to trespass upon their life—nay, they themselves even lead in those who will eventually possess it. No one is to be found who is willing to distribute his money, yet among how many does each one of us distribute his life! In guarding their fortune men are often closefisted, yet, when it comes to the matter of wasting time, in the case of the one thing in which it is right to be miserly, they show themselves most prodigal. And so I should like to lay hold upon someone from the company of older men and say: "I see that you have reached the farthest limit of human life, you are pressing hard upon your hundredth year, or are even beyond it; come now, recall your life and make a reckoning. Consider how much of your time was taken up with a moneylender, how much with a mistress, how much with a patron, how much with a client, how much in wrangling with your wife, how much in punishing your slaves, how much in rushing about the city on social duties. Add the diseases which we have caused by our own acts, add, too, the time that has lain idle and unused; you will see that you have fewer years to your credit than you count. Look back in memory and consider when you ever had a fixed plan, how few days have passed as you had intended, when you were ever at your own disposal, when your face ever wore its natural expression, when your mind was ever unperturbed, what work you have achieved in so long a life, how many have robbed you of life when you were not aware of what you were losing, how much was taken up in useless sorrow, in foolish joy, in greedy desire, in the allurements of society, how little of yourself was left to you; you will perceive that you are dying before your season!"[1] What, then, is the reason of this? You live as if you were destined to live forever, no thought of your frailty ever enters your head, of how much time has already gone by you take no heed. You squander time as if you drew from a full and abundant supply, though all the while that day which you bestow on some person or thing is perhaps your last. You have all the fears of mortals and all the desires of immortals. You will hear many men saying: "After my fiftieth year I shall retire into leisure, my sixtieth year shall release me from public duties." And what guarantee, pray, have you that your life will last longer? Who will suffer your course to be just as you plan it? Are you not ashamed to reserve for yourself only the remnant of life, and to set apart for wisdom only that time which cannot be devoted to any business? How late it is to begin to live just when we must cease to live! What foolish forgetfulness of mortality to postpone wholesome plans to the fiftieth and sixtieth year, and to intend to begin life at a point to which few have attained!

---

1. Literally, "unripe." At 100 he should "come to his grave in a full age, like as a shock of corn cometh in in his season" (Job v. 26); but he is still unripe.

CHAPTER FOUR

You will see that the most powerful and highly placed men let drop remarks in which they long for leisure, acclaim it, and prefer it to all their blessings. They desire at times, if it could be with safety, to descend from their high pinnacle; for, though nothing from without should assail or shatter, Fortune of its very self comes crashing down[1].

The deified Augustus, to whom the gods vouchsafed more than to any other man, did not cease to pray for rest and to seek release from public affairs; all his conversation ever reverted to this subject—his hope of leisure. This was the sweet, even if vain, consolation with which he would gladden his labours—that he would one day live for himself. In a letter addressed to the senate, in which he had promised that his rest would not be devoid of dignity nor inconsistent with his former glory, I find these words: "But these matters can be shown better by deeds than by promises. Nevertheless, since the joyful reality is still far distant, my desire for that time most earnestly prayed for has led me to forestall some of its delight by the pleasure of words." So desirable a thing did leisure seem that he anticipated it in thought because he could not attain it in reality. He who saw everything depending upon himself alone, who determined the fortune of individuals and of nations, thought most happily of that future day on which he should lay aside his greatness. He had discovered how much sweat those blessings that shone throughout all lands drew forth, how many secret worries they concealed. Forced to pit arms first against his countrymen, then against his colleagues, and lastly against his relatives, he shed blood on land and sea.

Through Macedonia, Sicily, Egypt, Syria, and Asia, and almost all countries he followed the path of battle, and when his troops were weary of shedding Roman blood, he turned them to foreign wars. While he was pacifying the Alpine regions, and subduing the enemies planted in the midst of a peaceful empire, while he was extending its bounds even beyond the Rhine and the Euphrates and the Danube, in Rome itself the swords of Murena, Caepio, Lepidus, Egnatius, and others were being whetted to slay him. Not yet had he escaped their plots, when his daughter[2] and all the noble youths who were bound to her by adultery as by a sacred oath, oft alarmed his failing years—and there was Paulus, and a second time the need to fear a woman in league with an Antony.[3] When be had cut away these ulcers[4] together with the limbs themselves, others would grow in their place; just as in a body that was overburdened with blood, there was always a rupture somewhere. And so he longed for leisure, in the hope and thought of which he found relief for his labours. This was the prayer of one who was able to answer the prayers of mankind.

---

1. The idea is that greatness sinks beneath its own weight. *Cf.* Seneca, *Agamemnon*, **88** *sq.*:
    Sidunt ipso pondere magna
    ceditque oneri Fortuna suo.
2. The notorious Julia, who was banished by Augustus to the island of Pandataria.
3. In 31 B.C. Augustus had been pitted against Mark Antony and Cleopatra; in 2 B.C. Iullus Antonius, younger son of the triumvir, was sentenced to death by reason of his intrigue with the elder Julia.
4. The language is reminiscent of Augustus's own characterization of Julia and his two grandchildren in Suetonius (*Aug.* 65. 5): "nec (solebat) aliter eos appellare quam tris vomicas ac tria carcinomata sua" ("his trio of boils and trio of ulcers").

CHAPTER FIVE

Marcus Cicero, long flung among men like Catiline and Clodius and Pompey and Crassus, some open enemies, others doubtful friends, as he is tossed to and fro along with the state and seeks to keep it from destruction, to be at last swept away, unable as he was to be restful in prosperity or patient in adversity—how many times does he curse that very consulship of his, which he had lauded without end, though not without reason! How tearful the words he uses in a letter[1] written to Atticus, when Pompey the elder had been conquered, and the son was still trying to restore his shattered arms in Spain! "Do you ask," he said, "what I am doing here? I am lingering in my Tusculan villa half a prisoner." He then proceeds to other statements, in which he bewails his former life and complains of the present and despairs of the future. Cicero said that he was "half a prisoner." But, in very truth, never will the wise man resort to so lowly a term, never will he be half a prisoner—he who always possesses an undiminished and stable liberty, being free and his own master and towering over all others. For what can possibly be above him who is above Fortune?

---

1. Not extant.

CHAPTER SIX

When Livius Drusus,[1] a bold and energetic man, had with the support of a huge crowd drawn from all Italy proposed new laws and the evil measures of the Gracchi, seeing no way out for his policy, which he could neither carry through nor abandon when once started on, he is said to have complained bitterly against the life of unrest he had had from the cradle, and to have exclaimed that he was the only person who had never had a holiday even as a boy. For, while he was still a ward and wearing the dress of a boy, he had had the courage to commend to the favour of a jury those who were accused, and to make his influence felt in the law-courts, so powerfully, indeed, that it is very well known that in certain trials he forced a favourable verdict. To what lengths was not such premature ambition destined to go? One might have known that such precocious hardihood would result in great personal and public misfortune. And so it was too late for him to complain that he had never had a holiday when from boyhood he had been a trouble-maker and a nuisance in the forum. It is a question whether he died by his own hand; for he fell from a sudden wound received in his groin, some doubting whether his death was voluntary, no one, whether it was timely.

It would be superfluous to mention more who, though others deemed them the happiest of men, have expressed their loathing for every act of their years, and with their own lips have given true testimony against themselves; but by these complaints they changed neither themselves nor others. For when they have vented their feelings in words, they fall back into their usual round. Heaven knows! such lives as yours, though they should pass the limit of a thousand years, will shrink into the merest span; your vices will swallow up any amount of time. The space you have, which reason can prolong, although it naturally hurries away, of necessity escapes from you quickly; for you do not seize it, you neither hold it back, nor impose delay upon the swiftest thing in the world, but you allow it to slip away as if it were something superfluous and that could be replaced.

---

1. As tribune in 91 B.C. he proposed a corn law and the granting of citizenship to the Italians.

CHAPTER SEVEN

But among the worst I count also those who have time for nothing but wine and lust; for none have more shameful engrossments.[1] The others, even if they are possessed by the empty dream of glory, nevertheless go astray in a seemly manner; though you should cite to me the men who are avaricious, the men who are wrathful, whether busied with unjust hatreds or with unjust wars, these all sin in more manly fashion. But those who are plunged into the pleasures of the belly and into lust bear a stain that is dishonourable. Search into the hours of all these people,[2] see how much time they give to accounts, how much to laying snares, how much to fearing them, how much to paying court, how much to being courted, how much is taken up in giving or receiving bail, how much by banquets—for even these have now become a matter of business—, and you will see how their interests, whether you call them evil or good, do not allow them time to breathe.

Finally, everybody agrees that no one pursuit can be successfully followed by a man who is busied with many things—eloquence cannot, nor the liberal studies—since the mind, when its interests are divided, takes in nothing very deeply, but rejects everything that is, as it were, crammed into it. There is nothing the busy man is less busied with than living: there is nothing that is harder to learn. Of the other arts there are many teachers everywhere; some of them we have seen that mere boys have mastered so thoroughly that they could even play the master. It takes the whole of life to learn how to live, and—what will perhaps make you wonder more—it takes the whole of life to learn how to die. Many very great men, having laid aside all their encumbrances, having renounced riches, business, and pleasures, have made it their one aim up to the very end of life to know how to live; yet the greater number of them have departed from life confessing that they did not yet know—still less do those others know. Believe me, it takes a great man and one who has risen far above human weaknesses not to allow any of his time to be filched from him, and it follows that the life of such a man is very long because he has devoted wholly to himself whatever time he has had. None of it lay neglected and idle; none of it was under the control of another, for, guarding it most grudgingly, he found nothing that was worthy to be taken in exchange for his time. And so that man had time enough, but those who have been robbed of much of their life by the public, have necessarily had too little of it.

And there is no reason for you to suppose that these people are not sometimes aware of their loss. Indeed, you will hear many of those who are burdened by great prosperity cry out at times in the midst of their throngs of clients, or their pleadings in court, or their other glorious miseries: "I have no chance to live." Of course you have no chance! All those who summon you to themselves, turn you away from your own self. Of how many days has that defendant robbed you? Of how many that candidate? Of how many that old woman wearied with burying her heirs?[3] Of how many that man who is shamming sickness for the purpose of exciting the greed of the legacy-hunters? Of how many that very powerful friend who has you and your like on the list, not of his friends, but of his retinue? Check off, I say, and review the days of your life; you will see that very few, and those the refuse, have been left for you. That man who had prayed for the fasces,[4] when he attains them, desires to lay them aside and says over and over: "When will this year be over!" That man gives games,[5] and, after setting great value on gaining the chance to give them, now says: "When shall I be rid of them?" That advocate is lionized throughout the whole forum, and fills all the place with a great crowd that stretches farther than he can be heard, yet he says: "When will vacation time come?" Everyone hurries his life on and suffers from a yearning for the future and a weariness of the present. But he who bestows all of his time on his own needs, who plans out every day as if it were his last, neither longs for nor fears the morrow. For what new pleasure is there that any hour can now bring? They are all known, all have been enjoyed to the full. Mistress Fortune may deal out the rest as she likes; his life has already found safety. Something may be added to it, but nothing taken from it, and he will take any addition as the man who is satisfied and filled takes the food which he does not desire and yet can hold. And so there is no reason for you to think that any man has lived long because he has grey hairs or wrinkles; he has not lived long— he has existed long. For what if you should think that that man had had a long voyage who had been caught by a fierce storm as soon as he left harbour, and, swept hither and thither by a succession of winds that raged from different quarters, had been driven in a circle around the same course? Not much voyaging did he have, but much tossing about.

---

1. Throughout the essay *occupati*, "the engrossed," is a technical term designating those who are so absorbed in the interests of life that they take no time for philosophy.
2. *i.e.*, the various types of *occupati* that have been sketchily presented. The looseness of the structure has led some editors to doubt the integrity of the passage.
3. *i.e.*, she has become the prey of legacy-hunters.
4. The rods that were the symbol of high office.
5. At this time the management of the public games was committed to the praetors.

CHAPTER EIGHT

I am often filled with wonder when I see some men demanding the time of others and those from whom they ask it most indulgent. Both of them fix their eyes on the object of the request for time, neither of them on the time itself; just as if what is asked were nothing, what is given, nothing. Men trifle with the most precious thing in the world; but they are blind to it because it is an incorporeal thing, because it does not come beneath the sight of the eyes, and for this reason it is counted a very cheap thing—nay, of almost no value at all. Men set very great store by pensions and doles, and for these they hire out their labour or service or effort. But no one sets a value on time; all use it lavishly as if it cost nothing. But see how these same people clasp the knees of physicians if they fall ill and the danger of death draws nearer, see how ready they are, if threatened with capital punishment, to spend all their possessions in order to live! So great is the inconsistency of their feelings. But if each one could have the number of his future years set before him as is possible in the case of the years that have passed, how alarmed those would be who saw only a few remaining, how sparing of them would they be! And yet it is easy to dispense an amount that is assured, no matter how small it may be; but that must be guarded more carefully which will fail you know not when.

Yet there is no reason for you to suppose that these people do not know how precious a thing time is; for to those whom they love most devotedly they have a habit of saying that they are ready to give them a part of their own years. And they do give it, without realizing it; but the result of their giving is that they themselves suffer loss without adding to the years of their dear ones. But the very thing they do not know is whether they are suffering loss; therefore, the removal of something that is lost without being noticed they find is bearable. Yet no one will bring back the years, no one will bestow you once more on yourself. Life will follow the path it started upon, and will neither reverse nor check its course; it will make no noise, it will not remind you of its swiftness. Silent it will glide on; it will not prolong itself at the command of a king, or at the applause of the populace. Just as it was started on its first day, so it will run; nowhere will it turn aside, nowhere will it delay. And what will be the result? You have been engrossed, life hastens by; meanwhile death will be at hand, for which, willy nilly, you must find leisure.

CHAPTER NINE

Can anything be sillier than the point of view of certain people—I mean those who boast of their foresight? They keep themselves very busily engaged in order that they may be able to live better; they spend life in making ready to live! They form their purposes with a view to the distant future; yet postponement is the greatest waste of life; it deprives them of each day as it comes, it snatches from them the present by promising something hereafter. The greatest hindrance to living is expectancy, which depends upon the morrow and wastes to-day. You dispose of that which lies in the hands of Fortune, you let go that which lies in your own. Whither do you look? At what goal do you aim? All things that are still to come lie in uncertainty; live straightway! See how the greatest of bards cries out, and, as if inspired with divine utterance, sings the saving strain:

The fairest day in hapless mortals' life
Is ever first to flee.[1]

"Why do you delay," says he, "Why are you idle? Unless you seize the day, it flees." Even though you seize it, it still will flee; therefore you must vie with time's swiftness in the speed of using it, and, as from a torrent that rushes by and will not always flow, you must drink quickly. And, too, the utterance of the bard is most admirably worded to cast censure upon infinite delay, in that he says, not "the fairest age," but "the fairest day." Why, to whatever length your greed inclines, do you stretch before yourself months and years in long array, unconcerned and slow though time flies so fast? The poet speaks to you about the day, and about this very day that is flying. Is there, then, any doubt that for hapless mortals, that is, for men who are engrossed, the fairest day is ever the first to flee? Old age surprises them while their minds are still childish, and they come to it unprepared and unarmed, for they have made no provision for it; they have stumbled upon it suddenly and unexpectedly, they did not notice that it was drawing nearer day by day. Even as conversation or reading or deep meditation on some subject beguiles the traveller, and he finds that he has reached the end of his journey before he was aware that he was approaching it, just so with this unceasing and most swift journey of life, which we make at the same pace whether waking or sleeping; those who are engrossed become aware of it only at the end.

---

1. Virgil, *Georgics*, iii. 66 *sq*.

CHAPTER TEN

Should I choose to divide my subject into heads with their separate proofs, many arguments will occur to me by which I could prove that busy men find life very short. But Fabianus,[1] who was none of your lecture-room philosophers of to-day, but one of the genuine and old-fashioned kind, used to say that we must fight against the passions with main force, not with artifice, and that the battle-line must be turned by a bold attack, not by inflicting pinpricks; that sophistry is not serviceable, for the passions must be, not nipped, but crushed. Yet, in order that the victims of them nay be censured, each for his own particular fault, I say that they must be instructed, not merely wept over.

Life is divided into three periods—that which has been, that which is, that which will be. Of these the present time is short, the future is doubtful, the past is certain. For the last is the one over which Fortune has lost control, is the one which cannot be brought back under any man's power. But men who are engrossed lose this; for they have no time to look back upon the past, and even if they should have, it is not pleasant to recall something they must view with regret. They are, therefore, unwilling to direct their thoughts backward to ill-spent hours, and those whose vices become obvious if they review the past, even the vices which were disguised under some allurement of momentary pleasure, do not have the courage to revert to those hours. No one willingly turns his thought back to the past, unless all his acts have been submitted to the censorship of his conscience, which is never deceived; he who has ambitiously coveted, proudly scorned, recklessly conquered, treacherously betrayed, greedily seized, or lavishly squandered, must needs fear his own memory. And yet this is the part of our time that is sacred and set apart, put beyond the reach of all human mishaps, and removed from the dominion of Fortune, the part which is disquieted by no want, by no fear, by no attacks of disease; this can neither be troubled nor be snatched away—it is an everlasting and unanxious possession. The present offers only one day at a time, and each by minutes; but all the days of past time will appear when you bid them, they will suffer you to behold them and keep them at your will—a thing which those who are engrossed have no time to do. The mind that is untroubled and tranquil has the power to roam into all the parts of its life; but the minds of the engrossed, just as if weighted by a yoke, cannot turn and look behind. And so their life vanishes into an abyss; and as it does no good, no matter how much water you pour into a vessel, if there is no bottom² to receive and hold it, so with time—it makes no difference how much is given; if there is nothing for it to settle upon, it passes out through the chinks and holes of the mind. Present time is very brief, so brief, indeed, that to some there seems to be none; for it is always in motion, it ever flows and hurries on; it ceases to be before it has come, and can no more brook delay than the firmament or the stars, whose ever unresting movement never lets them abide in the same track. The engrossed, therefore, are concerned with present time alone, and it is so brief that it cannot be grasped, and even this is filched away from them, distracted as they are among many things.

---

1. A much admired teacher of Seneca.
2. An allusion to the fate of the Danaids, who in Hades forever poured water into a vessel with a perforated bottom.

CHAPTER ELEVEN

In a word, do you want to know how they do not "live long"? See how eager they are to live long! Decrepit old men beg in their prayers for the addition of a few more years; they pretend that they are younger than they are; they comfort themselves with a falsehood, and are as pleased to deceive themselves as if they deceived Fate at the same time. But when at last some infirmity has reminded them of their mortality, in what terror do they die, feeling that they are being dragged out of life, and not merely leaving it. They cry out that they have been fools, because they have not really lived, and that they will live henceforth in leisure if only they escape from this illness; then at last they reflect how uselessly they have striven for things which they did not enjoy, and how all their toil has gone for nothing. But for those whose life is passed remote from all business, why should it not be ample? None of it is assigned to another, none of it is scattered in this direction and that, none of it is committed to Fortune, none of it perishes from neglect, none is subtracted by wasteful giving, none of it is unused; the whole of it, so to speak, yields income. And so, however small the amount of it, it is abundantly sufficient, and therefore, whenever his last day shall come, the wise man will not hesitate to go to meet death with steady step.

CHAPTER TWELVE

Perhaps you ask whom I would call "the engrossed"? There is no reason for you to suppose that I mean only those whom the dogs[1] that have at length been let in drive out from the law-court, those whom you see either gloriously crushed in their own crowd of followers, or scornfully in someone else's, those whom social duties call forth from their own homes to bump them against someone else's doors, or whom the praetor's hammer[2] keeps busy in seeking gain that is disreputable and that will one day fester. Even the leisure of some men is engrossed; in their villa or on their couch, in the midst of solitude, although they have withdrawn from all others, they are themselves the source of their own worry; we should say that these are living, not in leisure, but in busy idleness.[3] Would you say that that man is at leisure[4] who arranges with finical care his Corinthian bronzes, that the mania of a few makes costly, and spends the greater part of each day upon rusty bits of copper? Who sits in a public wrestling-place (for, to our shame I we labour with vices that are not even Roman) watching the wrangling of lads? Who sorts out the herds of his pack-mules into pairs of the same age and colour? Who feeds all the newest athletes? Tell me, would you say that those men are at leisure who pass many hours at the barber's while they are being stripped of whatever grew out the night before? while a solemn debate is held over each separate hair? while either disarranged locks are restored to their place or thinning ones drawn from this side and that toward the forehead? How angry they get if the barber has been a bit too careless, just as if he were shearing a real man! How they flare up if any of their mane is lopped off, if any of it lies out of order, if it does not all fall into its proper ringlets! Who of these would not rather have the state disordered than his hair? Who is not more concerned to have his head trim rather than safe? Who would not rather be well barbered than upright? Would you say that these are at leisure who are occupied with the comb and the mirror? And what of those who are engaged in composing, hearing, and learning songs, while they twist the voice, whose best and simplest movement Nature designed to be straightforward, into the meanderings of some indolent tune, who are always snapping their fingers as they beat time to some song they have in their head, who are overheard humming a tune when they have been summoned to serious, often even melancholy, matters? These have not leisure, but idle occupation. And their banquets, Heaven knows! I cannot reckon among their unoccupied hours, since I see how anxiously they set out their silver plate, how diligently they tie up the tunics of their pretty slave-boys, how breathlessly they watch to see in what style the wild boar issues from the hands of the cook, with what speed at a given signal smooth-faced boys hurry to perform their duties, with what skill the birds are carved into portions all according to rule, how carefully unhappy little lads wipe up the spittle of drunkards. By such means they seek the reputation of being fastidious and elegant, and to such an extent do their evils follow them into all the privacies of life that they can neither eat nor drink without ostentation. And I would not count these among the leisured class either—the men who have themselves borne hither and thither in a sedan-chair and a litter, and are punctual at the hours for their rides as if it were unlawful to omit them, who are reminded by someone else when they must bathe, when they must swim, when they must dine; so enfeebled are they by the excessive lassitude of a pampered mind that they cannot find out by themselves whether they are hungry! I hear that one of these pampered people—provided that you can call it pampering to unlearn the habits of human life—when he had been lifted by hands from the bath and placed in his sedan-chair, said questioningly: "Am I now seated?" Do you think that this man, who does not know whether he is sitting, knows whether he is alive, whether he sees, whether he is at leisure? I find it hard to say whether I pity him more if he really did not know, or if he pretended not to know this. They really are subject to forgetfulness of many things, but they also pretend forgetfulness of many. Some vices delight them as being proofs of their prosperity; it seems the part of a man who is very lowly and despicable to know what he is doing. After this imagine that the mimes[5] fabricate many things to make a mock of luxury! In very truth, they pass over more than they invent, and such a multitude of unbelievable vices has come forth in this age, so clever in this one direction, that by now we can charge the mimes with neglect. To think that there is anyone who is so lost in luxury that he takes another's word as to whether he is sitting down! This man, then, is not at leisure, you must apply to him a different term—he is sick, nay, he is dead; that man is at leisure, who has also a perception of his leisure. But this other who is half alive, who, in order that he may know the postures of his own body, needs someone to tell him—how can he be the master of any of his time?

---

1. Apparently watch-dogs that were let in at nightfall, and caught the engrossed lawyer still at his task.
2. Literally, "spear," which was stuck in the ground as the sign of a public auction where captured or confiscated goods were put up for sale.
3. *Cf.* Pliny, *Epistles*, i. 9. 8: "satius est enim, ut Atilius noster eruditissime simul et facetissime dixit, otiosum esse quam nihil agere."
4. For the technical meaning of *otiosi*, "the leisured," see Seneca's definition at the beginning of chap. 14.
5. Actors in the popular mimes, or low farces, that were often censured for their indecencies.

CHAPTER THIRTEEN

It would be tedious to mention all the different men who have spent the whole of their life over chess or ball or the practice of baking their bodies in the sun. They are not unoccupied whose pleasures are made a busy occupation. For instance, no one will have any doubt that those are laborious triflers who spend their time on useless literary problems, of whom even among the Romans there is now a great number. It was once a foible confined to the Greeks to inquire into what number of rowers Ulysses had, whether the Iliad or the Odyssey was written first, whether moreover they belong to the same author, and various other matters of this stamp, which, if you keep them to yourself, in no way pleasure your secret soul, and, if you publish them, make you seem more of a bore than a scholar. But now this vain passion for learning useless things has assailed the Romans also. In the last few days I heard someone telling who was the first Roman general to do this or that; Duilius was the first who won a naval battle, Curius Dentatus was the first who had elephants led in his triumph. Still, these matters, even if they add nothing to real glory, are nevertheless concerned with signal services to the state; there will be no profit in such knowledge, nevertheless it wins our attention by reason of the attractiveness of an empty subject. We may excuse also those who inquire into this—who first induced the Romans to go on board ship. It was Claudius, and this was the very reason he was surnamed Caudex, because among the ancients a structure formed by joining together several boards was called a *caudex*, whence also the Tables of the Law are called *codices*,[1] and, in the ancient fashion, boats that carry provisions up the Tiber are even to-day called *codicariae*. Doubtless this too may have some point— the fact that Valerius Corvinus was the first to conquer Messana, and was the first of the family of the Valerii to bear the surname Messana because be had transferred the name of the conquered city to himself, and was later called Messala after the gradual corruption of the name in the popular speech. Perhaps you will permit someone to be interested also in this —the fact that Lucius Sulla was the first to exhibit loosed lions in the Circus, though at other times they were exhibited in chains, and that javelin-throwers were sent by King Bocchus to despatch them? And, doubtless, this too may find some excuse—but does it serve any useful purpose to know that Pompey was the first to exhibit the slaughter of eighteen elephants in the Circus, pitting criminals against them in a mimic battle? He, a leader of the state and one who, according to report, was conspicuous among the leaders[2] of old for the kindness of his heart, thought it a notable kind of spectacle to kill human beings after a new fashion. Do they fight to the death? That is not enough! Are they torn to pieces? That is not enough! Let them be crushed by animals of monstrous bulk! Better would it be that these things pass into oblivion lest hereafter some all-powerful man should learn them and be jealous of an act that was nowise human.[3] O, what blindness does great prosperity cast upon our minds! When he was casting so many troops of wretched human beings to wild beasts born under a different sky, when he was proclaiming war between creatures so ill matched, when he was shedding so much blood before the eyes of the Roman people, who itself was soon to be forced to shed more. he then believed that he was beyond the power of Nature. But later this same man, betrayed by Alexandrine treachery, offered himself to the dagger of the vilest slave, and then at last discovered what an empty boast his surname[4] was.

But to return to the point from which I have digressed, and to show that some people bestow useless pains upon these same matters—the man I mentioned related that Metellus, when he triumphed after his victory over the Carthaginians in Sicily, was the only one of all the Romans who had caused a hundred and twenty captured elephants to be led before his car; that Sulla was the last of the Roman's who extended the *pomerium*,[5] which in old times it was customary to extend after the acquisition of Italian but never of provincial, territory. Is it more profitable to know this than that Mount Aventine, according to him, is outside the *pomerium* for one of two reasons, either because that was the place to which the plebeians had seceded, or because the birds had not been favourable when Remus took his auspices on that spot—and, in turn, countless other reports that are either crammed with falsehood or are of the same sort? For though you grant that they tell these things in good faith, though they pledge themselves for the truth of what they write, still whose mistakes will be made fewer by such stories? Whose passions will they restrain? Whom will they make more brave, whom more just, whom more noble-minded? My friend Fabianus used to say that at times he was doubtful whether it was not better not to apply oneself to any studies than to become entangled in these.

---

1. The ancient codex was made of tablets of wood fastened together.
2. Such, doubtless, as Marius, Sulla, Caesar, Crassus.
3. Pliny (*Nat. Hist.* viii. 21) reports that the people were so moved by pity that they rose in a body and called down curses upon Pompey. Cicero's impressions of the occasion are recorded in *Ad Fam.* vii. 1. 3: "extremus elephantorum dies fuit, in quo admiratio magna vulgi atque turbae, delectatio nulla exstitit; quin etiam misericordia quaedam consecuta est atque opinio eiusmodi, esse quandam illi beluae cum genere humana societatem."
4. *i.e., Magnus.*
5. A name applied to a consecrated space kept vacant within and (according to Livy, i. 44) without the city wall. The right of extending it belonged originally to the king who had added territory to Rome.

CHAPTER FOURTEEN

Of all men they alone are at leisure who take time for philosophy, they alone really live; for they are not content to be good guardians of their own lifetime only. They annex ever age to their own; all the years that have gone ore them are an addition to their store. Unless we are most ungrateful, all those men, glorious fashioners of holy thoughts, were born for us; for us they have prepared a way of life. By other men's labours we are led to the sight of things most beautiful that have been wrested from darkness and brought into light; from no age are we shut out, we have access to all ages, and if it is our wish, by greatness of mind, to pass beyond the narrow limits of human weakness, there is a great stretch of time through which we may roam. We may argue with Socrates, we may doubt[1] with Carneades, find peace with Epicurus, overcome human nature with the Stoics, exceed it with the Cynics. Since Nature allows us to enter into fellowship with every age, why should we not turn from this paltry and fleeting span of time and surrender ourselves with all our soul to the past, which is boundless, which is eternal, which we share with our betters?

Those who rush about in the performance of social duties, who give themselves and others no rest, when they have fully indulged their madness, when they have every day crossed everybody's threshold, and have left no open door unvisited, when they have carried around their venal greeting to houses that are very far apart—out of a city so huge and torn by such varied desires, how few will they be able to see? How many will there be who either from sleep or self-indulgence or rudeness will keep them out! How many who, when they have tortured them with long waiting, will rush by, pretending to be in a hurry! How many will avoid passing out through a hall that is crowded with clients, and will make their escape through some concealed door as if it were not more discourteous to deceive than to exclude. How many, still half asleep and sluggish from last night's debauch, scarcely lifting their lips in the midst of a most insolent yawn, manage to bestow on yonder poor wretches, who break their own slumber[2] in order to wait on that of another, the right name only after it has been whispered to them a thousand times!

But we may fairly say that they alone are engaged in the true duties of life who shall wish to have Zeno, Pythagoras, Democritus, and all the other high priests of liberal studies, and Aristotle and Theophrastus, as their most intimate friends every day. No one of these will be "not at home," no one of these will fail to have his visitor leave more happy and more devoted to himself than when he came, no one of these will allow anyone to leave him with empty hands; all mortals can meet with them by night or by day.

---

1. The New Academy taught that certainty of knowledge was unattainable.
2. The *salutatio* was held in the early morning.

CHAPTER FIFTEEN

No one of these will force you to die, but all will teach you how to die; no one of these will wear out your years, but each will add his own years to yours; conversations with no one of these will bring you peril, the friendship of none will endanger your life, the courting of none will tax your purse. From them you will take whatever you wish; it will be no fault of theirs if you do not draw the utmost that you can desire. What happiness, what a fair old age awaits him who has offered himself as a client to these! He will have friends from whom he may seek counsel on matters great and small, whom he may consult every day about himself, from whom he may hear truth without insult, praise without flattery, and after whose likeness he may fashion himself.

We are wont to say that it was not in our power to choose the parents who fell to our lot, that they have been given to men by chance; yet *we* may be the sons of whomsoever we will. Households there are of noblest intellects; choose the one into which you wish to be adopted; you will inherit not merely their name, but even their property, which there will be no need to guard in a mean or niggardly spirit; the more persons you share it with, the greater it will become. These will open to you the path to immortality, and will raise you to a height from which no one is cast down. This is the only way of prolonging mortality—nay, of turning it into immortality. Honours, monuments, all that ambition has commanded by decrees or reared in works of stone, quickly sink to ruin; there is nothing that the lapse of time does not tear down and remove. But the works which philosophy has consecrated cannot be harmed; no age will destroy them, no age reduce them; the following and each succeeding age will but increase the reverence for them, since envy works upon what is close at hand, and things that are far off we are more free to admire. The life of the philosopher, therefore, has wide range, and he is not confined by the same bounds that shut others in. He alone is freed from the limitations of the human race; all ages serve him as if a god. Has some time passed by? This he embraces by recollection. Is time present? This he uses. Is it still to come? This he anticipates. He makes his life long by combining all times into one.

CHAPTER SIXTEEN

But those who forget the past, neglect the present, and fear for the future have a life that is very brief and troubled; when they have reached the end of it, the poor wretches perceive too late that for such a long while they have been busied in doing nothing. Nor because they sometimes invoke death, have you any reason to think it any proof that they find life long. In their folly they are harassed by shifting emotions which rush them into the very things they dread; they often pray for death because they fear it. And, too, you have no reason to think that this is any proof that they are living a long time—the fact that the day often seems to them long, the fact that they complain that the hours pass slowly until the time set for dinner arrives; for, whenever their engrossments fail them, they are restless because they are left with nothing to do, and they do not know how to dispose of their leisure or to drag out the time. And so they strive for something else to occupy them, and all the intervening time is irksome; exactly as they do when a gladiatorial exhibition\b is been announced, or when they are waiting for the appointed time of some other show or amusement, they want to skip over the days that lie between. All postponement of something they hope for seems long to them. Yet the time which they enjoy is short and swift, and it is made much shorter by their own fault; for they flee from one pleasure to another and cannot remain fixed in one desire. Their days are not long to them, but hateful; yet, on the other hand, how scanty seem the nights which they spend in the arms of a harlot or in wine! It is this also that accounts for the madness of poets in fostering human frailties by the tales in which they represent that Jupiter under the enticement of the pleasures of a lover doubled the length of the night. For what is it but to inflame our vices to inscribe the name of the gods as their sponsors, and to present the excused indulgence of divinity as an example to our own weakness? Can the nights which they pay for so dearly fail to seem all too short to these men? They lose the day in expectation of the night, and the night in fear of the dawn.

CHAPTER SEVENTEEN

The very pleasures of such men are uneasy and disquieted by alarms of various sorts, and at the very moment of rejoicing the anxious thought comes over them: How long will these things last?" This feeling has led kings to weep over the power they possessed, and they have not so much delighted in the greatness of their fortune, as they have viewed with terror the end to which it must some time come. When the King of Persia,[1] in all the insolence of his pride, spread his army over the vast plains and could not grasp its number but simply its measure,[2] he shed copious tears because inside of a hundred years not a man of such a mighty army would be alive.[3] But he who wept was to bring upon them their fate, was to give some to their doom on the sea, some on the land, some in battle, some in flight, and within a short time was to destroy all those for whose hundredth year he had such fear. And why is it that even their joys are uneasy from fear? Because they do not rest on stable causes, but are perturbed as groundlessly as they are born. But of what sort do you think those times are which even by their own confession are wretched, since even the joys by which they are exalted and lifted above mankind are by no means pure? All the greatest blessings are a source of anxiety, and at no time is fortune less wisely trusted than when it is best; to maintain prosperity there is need of other prosperity, and in behalf of the prayers that have turned out well we must make still other prayers. For everything that comes to us from chance is unstable, and the higher it rises, the more liable it is to fall. Moreover, what is doomed to perish brings pleasure to no one; very wretched, therefore, and not merely short, must the life of those be who work hard to gain what they must work harder to keep. By great toil they attain what they wish, and with anxiety hold what they have attained; meanwhile they take no account of time that will never more return. New engrossments take the place of the old, hope leads to new hope, ambition to new ambition. They do not seek an end of their wretchedness, but change the cause. Have we been tormented by our own public honours? Those of others take more of our time. Have we ceased to labour as candidates? We begin to canvass for others. Have we got rid of the troubles of a prosecutor? We find those of a judge. Has a man ceased to be a judge? He becomes president of a court. Has he become infirm in managing the property of others at a salary? He is perplexed by caring for his own wealth. Have the barracks [4]set Marius free? The consulship keeps him busy. Does Quintius[5] hasten to get to the end of his dictatorship? He will be called back to it from the plough. Scipio will go against the Carthaginians before he is ripe for so great an undertaking; victorious over Hannibal, victorious over Antiochus, the glory of his own consulship, the surety for his brother's, did he not stand in his own way, he would be set beside Jove[6]; but the discord of civilians will vex their preserver, and, when as a young man he had scorned honours that rivalled those of the gods, at length, when he is old, his ambition will lake delight in stubborn exile.[7] Reasons for anxiety will never be lacking, whether born of prosperity or of wretchedness; life pushes on in a succession of engrossments. We shall always pray for leisure, but never enjoy it.

---

1. Xerxes, who invaded Greece in 480 B.C.
2. On the plain of Doriscus in Thrace the huge land force was estimated by counting the number of times a space capable of holding 10,000 men was filled (Herodotus, vii. 60).
3. Herodotus, vii. 45, 46 tells the story.
4. *Caliga*, the boot of the common soldier, is here synonymous with service in the army.
5. His first appointment was announced to him while he was ploughing his own fields.
6. He did not allow his statue to be placed in the Capitol.
7. Disgusted with politics, he died in exile at Liternum.

CHAPTER EIGHTEEN

And so, my dearest Paulinus, tear yourself away from the crowd, and, too much storm-tossed for the time you have lived, at length withdraw into a peaceful harbour. Think of how many waves you have encountered, how many storms, on the one hand, you have sustained in private life, how many, on the other, you have brought upon yourself in public life; long enough has your virtue been displayed in laborious and unceasing proofs—try how it will behave in leisure. The greater part of your life, certainly the better part of it, has been given to the state; take now some part of your time for yourself as well. And I do not summon you to slothful or idle inaction, or to drown all your native energy in slumbers and the pleasures that are dear to the crowd. That is not to rest; you will find far greater works than all those you have hitherto performed so energetically, to occupy you in the midst of your release and retirement. You, I know, manage the accounts of the whole world as honestly as you would a stranger's, as carefully as you would your own, as conscientiously as you would the state's. You win love in an office in which it is difficult to avoid hatred; but nevertheless believe me, it is better to have knowledge of the ledger of one's own life than of the corn-market. Recall that keen mind of yours, which is most competent to cope with the greatest subjects, from a service that is indeed honourable but hardly adapted to the happy life, and reflect that in all your training in the liberal studies, extending from your earliest years, you were not aiming at this—that it might be safe to entrust many thousand pecks of corn to your charge; you gave hope of something greater and more lofty. There will be no lack of men of tested worth and painstaking industry. But plodding oxen are much more suited to carrying heavy loads than thoroughbred horses, and who ever hampers the fleetness of such high-born creatures with a heavy pack? Reflect, besides, how much worry you have in subjecting yourself to such a great burden; your dealings are with the belly of man. A hungry people neither listens to reason, nor is appeased by justice, nor is bent by any entreaty. Very recently within those few day's after Gaius Caesar died—still grieving most deeply (if the dead have any feeling) because he knew that the Roman people were alive[1] and had enough food left for at any rate seven or eight days while he was building his bridges of boats[2] and playing with the resources of the empire, we were threatened with the worst evil that can befall men even during a siege—the lack of provisions; his imitation of a mad and foreign and misproud king[3] was very nearly at the cost of the city's destruction and famine and the general revolution that follows famine. What then must have been the feeling of those who had charge of the corn-market, and had to face stones, the sword, fire—and a Caligula? By the greatest subterfuge they concealed the great evil that lurked in the vitals of the state—with good reason, you may be sure. For certain maladies must be treated while the patient is kept in ignorance; knowledge of their disease has caused the death of many.

---

1. Probably an allusion to the mad wish of Caligula: "utinam populus Romanus unam cervicem haberet!" (Suetonius, *Calig.* 30), cited in *De Ira*, iii. 19. 2. The logic of the whole passage suffers from the uncertainty of the text.
2. Three and a half miles long, reaching from Baiae to the mole of Puteoli (Suetonius, *Calig.* 19).
3. Xerxes, who laid a bridge over the Hellespont.

CHAPTER NINETEEN

Do you retire to these quieter, safer, greater things! Think you that it is just the same whether you are concerned in having corn from oversea poured into the granaries, unhurt either by the dishonesty or the neglect of those who transport it, in seeing that it does not become heated and spoiled by collecting moisture and tallies in weight and measure, or whether you enter upon these sacred and lofty studies with the purpose of discovering what substance, what pleasure, what mode of life, what shape God has; what fate awaits your soul; where Nature lays us to rest When we are freed from the body; what the principle is that upholds all the heaviest matter in the centre of this world, suspends the light on high, carries fire to the topmost part, summons the stars to their proper changes—and ether matters, in turn, full of mighty wonders? You really must leave the ground and turn your mind's eye upon these things! Now while the blood is hot, we must enter with brisk step upon the better course. In this kind of life there awaits much that is good to know—the love and practice of the virtues, forgetfulness of the passions, knowledge of living and dying, and a life of deep repose.

The condition of all who are engrossed is wretched, but most wretched is the condition of those who labour at engrossments that are not even their own, who regulate their sleep by that of another, their walk by the pace of another, who are under orders in case of the freest things in the world—loving and hating. If these wish to know how short their life is, let them reflect how small a part of it is their own.

CHAPTER TWENTY

And so when you see a man often wearing the robe of office, when you see one whose name is famous in the Forum, do not envy him; those things are bought at the price of life. They will waste all their years, in order that they may have one year reckoned by their name.[1] Life has left some in the midst of their first struggles, before they could climb up to the height of their ambition; some, when they have crawled up through a thousand indignities to the crowning dignity, have been possessed by the unhappy thought that they have but toiled for an inscription on a tomb; some who have come to extreme old age, while they adjusted it to new hopes as if it were youth, have had it fail from sheer weakness in the midst of their great and shameless endeavours. Shameful is he whose breath leaves him in the midst of a trial when, advanced in years and still courting the applause of an ignorant circle, he is pleading for some litigant who is the veriest stranger; disgraceful is he who, exhausted more quickly by his mode of living than by his labour, collapses in the very midst of his duties; disgraceful is he who dies in the act of receiving payments on account, and draws a smile from his long delayed[2] heir. I cannot pass over an instance which occurs to me. Sextus[3] Turannius was an old man of long tested diligence, who, after his ninetieth year, having received release from the duties of his office by Gaius Caesar's own act, ordered himself to be laid out on his bed and to be mourned by the assembled household as if he were dead. The whole house bemoaned the leisure of its old master, and did not end its sorrow until his accustomed work was restored to him. Is it really such pleasure for a man to die in harness? Yet very many have the same feeling; their desire for their labour lasts longer than their ability; they fight against the weakness of the body, they judge old age to be a hardship on no other score than because it puts them aside. The law does not draft a soldier after his fiftieth year, it does not call a senator after his sixtieth; it is more difficult for men to obtain leisure from themselves than from the law. Meantime, while they rob and are being robbed, while they break up each other's repose, while they make each other wretched, their life is without profit, without pleasure, without any improvement of the mind. No one keeps death in view, no one refrains from far-reaching hopes; some men, indeed, even arrange for things that lie beyond life—huge masses of tombs and dedications of public works and gifts for their funeral-pyres and ostentatious funerals. But, in very truth, the funerals of such men ought to be conducted by the light of torches and wax tapers,[4] as though they had lived but the tiniest span.

---

1. The Roman year was dated by the names of the two annual consuls.
2. *i.e.*, long kept out of his inheritance.
3. Tacitus (*Annals*, i. 7) gives the *praenomen* as Gaius.
4. *i.e.*, as if they were children, whose funerals took place by night (Servius, *Aeneid*, xi. 143).

CONTENTS

Chapter 1	1
Chapter 2	4
Chapter 3	7
Chapter 4	10
Chapter 5	13
Chapter 6	15
Chapter 7	17
Chapter 8	21
Chapter 9	23
Chapter 10	26
Chapter 11	29
Chapter 12	31
Chapter 13	35
Chapter 14	39
Chapter 15	42
Chapter 16	44
Chapter 17	46
Chapter 18	49
Chapter 19	52
Chapter 20	54

Copyright © 2020 by FV Éditions
Translator : JW Basore
Hardcover ISBN : 979-10-299-0925-2
All Rights Reserved

www.ingramcontent.com/pod-product-compliance
Lightning Source LLC
LaVergne TN
LVHW042247070526
838201LV00089B/62